M3 Lee and Grant Medium T[...]

by David Doyle

Walk Around®

Squadron Signal Publications

Covers and art by Don Greer
Illustrations by Matheu Spraggins

Introduction

The M3 had its roots in the Ordnance Department's efforts of the late 1930s to develop a medium tank. By 1939, the M2 had been standardized and put into production at the Rock Island Arsenal. It featured an air-cooled radial engine, vertical volute spring suspension, and a high-velocity 37mm gun installed in a revolving turret. Development continued as the world crisis deepened. Improvements in the basic design led to the introduction of the M2A1 model, with thicker armor, a larger turret, and a more powerful radial engine. The M2A1 was to replace the M2 in production at Rock Island, but with the fall of France in the spring of 1940, it was recognized that the facilities at RIA were incapable of producing the numbers of medium tanks the government would now require. The Chrysler Corporation was approached, and by 15 August 1940, had agreed on a contract to produce 1,000 M2A1s in a government-financed, purpose-built tank arsenal.

Battlefield reports from Europe, however, indicated that the 37mm was no longer an adequate main gun. The newly established Armored Force stated that a 75mm gun would be required for the Army's medium tank. Two factors led to the tank as we know it. First, the Rock Island Arsenal engineers were allotted only 60 days to design the new vehicle. This meant that the engineers took the M2A1 as their basis and set about turning out an up-armored, up-gunned version, rather than an entirely new tank design. Secondly, a turret ring that would handle such a large (for the time) weapon did not then exist in the US, and there was not enough time to develop one. The result was the unusual design of the M3 Medium tank with its 75-mm main gun mounted in a sponson on the right front of the hull.

From the outset, the M3 was considered an interim design. The Ordnance Committee minutes of 29 August 1940 recognized the drawback of the sponson-mounted main gun, and included a statement that "the next step in this development would consist of relocating the 75mm gun in the turret – this tank to be put into production as soon as it is determined that the changes are satisfactory." Thus, at first the Armored Force recommended that production of the M3 be limited to a few hundred units, while awaiting development of the 75mm turret. Facing the need to equip the expanding US Army, as well as a devastated British armored force, however, it was decided to put the M3 into full production as soon as possible. The 1,000 M2A1s ordered in the Chrysler contract were immediately changed to M3s.

Rock Island Arsenal began construction of the M3 pilot, and close coordination was established with the various manufacturers in order to expedite production. Along with the Chrysler contract, the U.S. government placed initial orders for 685 units with the American Locomotive Works (ALCO) and the Baldwin Locomotive Works. Concurrently, the British government placed orders for 500 tanks with the Pullman Standard Car Company, 501 with the Pressed Steel Car Company, and 685 with Baldwin. Since the U.S. was not at war, initially the British contracts were purchased on a "Cash and Carry" basis. The only major change the British were permitted to make to the basic M3 design was the substitution of a larger cast turret capable of accommodating their No. 19 radio set in a bustle (U.S. practice at the time was to mount the radio on the hull). The British dubbed their version the "General Grant" and named the US-pattern tank the "General Lee."

Acknowledgments

This book would have been impossible without the generous help of Allan Cors and Marc Sehring at The National Museum of Americans in Wartime; Jacques Littlefield and the Military Vehicle Technology Foundation staff; David Fletcher at The Tank Museum, Bovington, Dorset; the Patton Museum staff; Kevin Sharp; Tom Kailbourn; Kurt Laughlin; and Joe DeMarco. Special thanks to Denise, who patiently traveled with me coast to coast as we photographed vehicles for this book. All photos are by the author unless otherwise stated.

About the Walk Around®/On Deck Series®

The Walk Around®/On Deck® series is about the details of specific military equipment using color and black-and-white archival photographs and photographs of in-service, preserved, and restored equipment. Walk Around® titles are devoted to aircraft and military vehicles, while On Deck® titles are devoted to warships. They are picture books of 80 pages, focusing on operational equipment, not one-off or experimental subjects.

Copyright 2008 Squadron/Signal Publications
1115 Crowley Drive, Carrollton, TX 75006-1312 U.S.A.
Printed in the U.S.A.

ISBN 978-0-89747-586-0

Military/Combat Photographs and Snapshots

If you have any photos of aircraft, armor, soldiers, or ships of any nation, particularly wartime snapshots, please share them with us and help make Squadron/Signal's books all the more interesting and complete in the future. Any photograph sent to us will be copied and returned. Electronic images are preferred. The donor will be fully credited for any photos used. Please send them to:

Squadron/Signal Publications
1115 Crowley Drive
Carrollton, TX 75006-1312 U.S.A.
www.SquadronSignalPublications.com

(Title Page) In an obviously posed photograph from World War II, the six-man crew of a U.S. Army M3 medium tank act out a desperate last-stand scenario, with revolvers and a Thompson submachine gun aimed at an imaginary oncoming enemy force. The driver's vision port and the pistol port in the side door are opening, revealing details of their inner sides and supports. Note the variations in color and shading of the G.I.s' one-piece herringbone twill overalls. (Library of Congress)

(Front Cover) A pair of M3 Medium Tanks in Commonwealth service stand abreast in North Africa. At right is an M3 Lee – designed for U.S. service, and at left is an M3 Grant – built for British service with its characteristic large turret.

(Back Cover) This column of M3s prepares to pull out while training at Ft. Knox. Road dust has coated the forward-facing surfaces of the tank - even the side door hinges - while leaving the sides of the vehicle relatively clean.

The M3 series of medium tanks were an outgrowth of this tank, the M2 medium. The M2 was armed with a high-velocity 37mm gun in a revolving turret, two fixed machine guns in the forward hull, four sponson-mounted machine guns, and two antiaircraft machine guns. The latter could be raised from positions just forward of the side doors. (TACOM LCMC History Office)

Here we see the last of 3,243 vehicles built at the Detroit Tank Arsenal. The placard on the M3 reads, "Chrysler M4 tanks crowd last M3 off the lines." Despite the radical difference in appearance of the two tanks, the M4 series was essentially built on the lower hull and running gear of the M3 series. The M3 builders had gained much experience producing the series, and the commonality of the M3 and M4 allowed for a rapid transition. Chrysler was very proud of the fact that it was able to switch production over to the M4 series "without losing a tank." The photograph is undated, but the last Chrysler-built M3 was accepted in August 1942. (Patton Museum)

Shown here is a Pullman-Standard built "General Grant." Produced for the British Purchasing Commission, the most evident difference from the U.S. model was the shape of the turret and lack of a commander's cupola. While U.S. practice of the time was to mount the radios in the hull, British practice required the wireless to be housed in the turret – hence the need for the larger turret. (Patton Museum, Fort Knox, Kentucky)

Battlefield reports from Europe indicated that the 37mm main gun of the M2 would no longer be adequate. The newly established Armored Force wanted a 75mm gun that would be required for the Army's medium tank, and gave the Rock Island Arsenal engineers only 60 days to design the new vehicle. Accordingly, the engineers set to work to produce an up-armored, up-gunned tank using the M2A1 as a basis. The turret ring that would handle such a large (for the time) weapon did not exist then in the US, and there was not enough time to develop one. Hence, the M3 Medium tanks had their 75-mm main gun mounted in a sponson on the right front of the hull. In this unusual view, an M3 takes flight during trials. (Patton Museum)

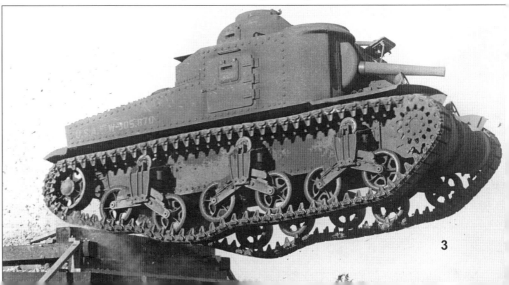

3

This M3 medium tank, belonging to the National Museum of Americans in Wartime, is a late-production vehicle manufactured by Chrysler at the Detroit Tank Arsenal in July 1942 and was originally given the U.S. Army registration number W-3058035. At some point the vehicle was turned over to the British. It was discovered a few years ago serving as a bulldozer in Australia, with a blade attached to the front and the turret removed. The tank subsequently was restored to its current excellent condition.

Among the characteristics of late-production Chrysler M3s on exhibit at the National Museum of Americans in Wartime are the long-barreled M3 cannon, the elimination of the side doors, and the horizontal ribs halfway up the outer faces of the bogie suspension brackets (sometimes referred to as frames), which are the large castings between each pair of road wheels. The front and center brackets of this vehicle exhibit that feature, while the rear bracket lacks the horizontal rib.

This drive sprocket is of the type used on M3s, a design that remained constant throughout the production run. Each drive sprocket assembly comprises a drum-shaped hub, to both sides of which are bolted 13-tooth sprockets. The hub, in turn, is bolted to eight studs on the outer face of the flange of the final drive. Casting numbers still appear on the bogie suspension bracket, but the road wheel edge shows deterioration.

Viewed from an angle, the hub of the left front drive sprocket is visible, as are some of the thirteen flanges surrounding the inner side of the hub, to which is bolted the inner sprocket. To the front of the road wheel at the right is the rear volute spring of the bogie.

The bogie assembly includes the suspension bracket, with the return roller mounted on top, and a road wheel suspended from twin arms at the front and back of the bracket. The levers (also called spring retainers) rest on wearing plates fastened to the tops of the arms and act in unison with the volute springs to cushion the ride. The arms are secured to the bottom of the bracket with pivots called suspension gudgeon pins.

From this angle, the volute spring of a bogie can be seen, along with its associated levers. The return roller at top exhibits an overspray of olive drab paint on the outer edge. Also apparent are two of the mounting bolts that secure the suspension bracket to the hull.

The idler wheels are also open, six-spoked in design, but without tires. Note the C199 part number cast on the hub cap.

The vehicle's original U.S. Army registration is painted on the hull sponson in matte blue drab paint. This was the color officially required for painting registration numbers until the last days of World War II. Details of the left rear suspension bracket, which lacks the horizontal ribs, are shown.

The end connectors of the T48 tracks also act as track guides. They are fastened to the pins of the track shoes by means of wedge bolts and locking nuts.

The M3's road wheels are six-spoked, with openings between each spoke. Each wheel is fitted with a 20-9 rubber tire. Lubricant staining can be seen on the wheel and the axle nut on this example. To the far right is the rear gudgeon pin of this bogie, which acts as an axle for the roadwheel.

7

The driver's front and side vision ports are open, revealing the protectoscopes (indirect vision devices with prism viewing blocks) on the inner sides. A bullet splash guard surrounds the opening of the side port. Note the row of slotted, oval-headed screws at the bottom of the front side plate, as contrasted by the rivets used on other plate-to-plate joints.

The two clips near the bottom of the front plate of the left upper hull were intended for storing a machine gun tripod.

This side view is of the left service headlight and blackout marker lamp. Surrounding them is a brush guard fabricated from welded metal strips and bolted to the fender. Electrical cables provide power to the lights.

A rear view of the left headlight and blackout marker lamp. Both lights are mounted on a common base with electrical connections. Braided jackets surround the electrical cables. Also visible to the left of the lights is the stiffener formed into the fender.

This is another view of the tripod storage clips. Once fully tightened, some of the screws were tack-welded in place. These small welds are visible at the top of each of the oval-headed screws along the bottom of the plate.

This is the left rear of the crew compartment. The bowl-shaped radio antenna mount has a casting number on the side. Note the single-slotted screw in the otherwise riveted angle iron joining the rear left plate of the compartment to the rear deck. Between that plate and the storage box are two armored fuel filler cap covers, the left one for the auxiliary generator fuel tank, and the right one for the left sponson fuel tank.

The antenna mount and auxiliary generator fuel filler cover are seen here close up. Projecting from the rear plate of the crew compartment, to the right of the antenna mount, is the housing for the external actuating handles of the fixed fire extinguisher system.

Details of the protectoscope mount on the interior side of the driver's side vision port are seen here. The splash guard is a bent strip of steel, with a built-up weld around the outside. Note the thickness of the armor at the port opening; the rolled homogenous steel is 1.5" thick here.

This view of the antenna mount also shows the forward latch of the storage box.

The left tail light assembly has two elements: a blackout light at the top, and a service light/service stop light below. The exterior actuating handles for the interior fixed fire extinguisher system and their housings are on the rear plate of the crew compartment, to the right of the storage box. The rectangular plate welded to the rear hull plate (right of center, toward bottom of photo) was an improvement on the earlier triangular support plates at that location.

The sides of the storage boxes are angled in order to make the sides of the box plumb and the lid level. Two hasp-type latches are fitted to the outside of the lid. A weld bead secures the box to the deck.

The electrical cable with its braided jacket is visible in this side view of the left tail light housing. The M3 used the standard U.S. military tail lights, which were different, depending on whether they were mounted on the left or right side of the vehicle.

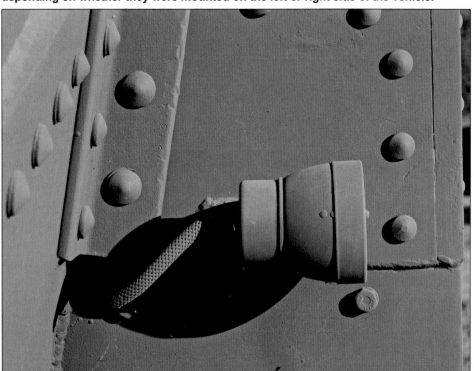

The engine compartment doors are open in this three-quarters left rear view of the M3 belonging to the National Museum of Americans in Wartime. There is an overhang at the top of the turret to accommodate the cupola ring. The shape of this overhang varied from vehicle to vehicle, with the contours where it blends into the turret's side being more or less noticeable.

This is a view over the rear deck of the M3. A pistol port with a protectoscope is on the right side of the rear plate of the crew compartment. On the forward center of the deck is a bracket for a shovel. The hole in the center of the rear plate of the hull toward the bottom of the photo is for the hand starter crank.

12

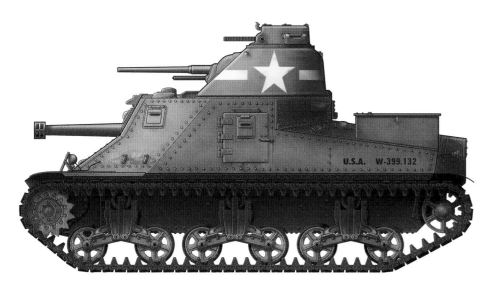

This First Armored Division M3 operated in Tunisia during November 1942, where this unit was badly bloodied.

This M3 is wears T48 tracks, a two-pin, rubber block, chevron-type tread, 16.56-inches wide, with 79 track shoes on each side. More common on the M3 was the T41 tread.

The storage boxes are hinged on the inner sides, with the top half of the hinge mounted on the inner side of the lid. A variety of brackets for mounting pioneer tools and a tow cable are on the engine deck. The fuel filler covers, one of which is to the rear of the pistol port, had no splash guard protection, and thus were vulnerable to projectiles.

Two large, slotted, oval-head screws secure the pistol port hinge to the hull at the right rear of the crew compartment. Protecting the sides of the port is a splash guard composed of a steel strip with a sloping weld bead built up against it. The rivet heads are conical, rather than round. There is a tool bracket clamping knob at the lower right.

Welded to the top of the right storage box lid are brackets for a hand crank for manually starting the engine. The handle of the crank would fit into the tube.

This is the housing of the spindle of the eccentric cam that adjusts the right idler wheel and track tension. To adjust the idler, the clamping bolts (the two outer hex bolts on the lower rear of the housing) are loosened, the spreading bolt (the center of the three bolts) is turned counterclockwise, the collar next to the large hex bolt at the inboard end of the split housing is pulled slightly toward the center of the vehicle, and the large hex bolt, connected to the end of the spindle shaft, is turned with an idler wrench.

The right oil-bath filter of the M3 is behind the rectangular plate welded to the underside of the rear overhang of the hull. Threaded rods and wing nuts hold the oil cup to the bottom of the assembly. Periodically, the cup was removed, cleaned, and refilled. In the shadow to the upper left is the outlet of the right engine exhaust outlet, or stub. The outlet is an elongated "fishtail" design with baffles.

This M3 at Fort Benning in April 1942 bears the national star insignia, as well as white bands around the turrets. The blue registration number on the tank at left is barely visible, in contrast to the plainly visible white "Geyser" name ahead of it.

14

On late-production vehicles with no side doors, like the M3 shown in this overall right side view, a pistol port was provided on the right side only.

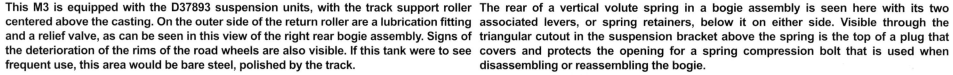

Faintly visible on the right idler wheel hub cap is a casting number. A lubrication fitting is on the side of the hub to the left of the top spoke.

This M3 is equipped with the D37893 suspension units, with the track support roller centered above the casting. On the outer side of the return roller are a lubrication fitting and a relief valve, as can be seen in this view of the right rear bogie assembly. Signs of the deterioration of the rims of the road wheels are also visible. If this tank were to see frequent use, this area would be bare steel, polished by the track.

A close-up of the right idler wheel, showing the burnished bare metal around the rim. The support bracket for the idler spindle housing is bolted to the hull next to the idler.

The rear of a vertical volute spring in a bogie assembly is seen here with its two associated levers, or spring retainers, below it on either side. Visible through the triangular cutout in the suspension bracket above the spring is the top of a plug that covers and protects the opening for a spring compression bolt that is used when disassembling or reassembling the bogie.

Unlike the road wheels, the track support rollers did not have rubber tires. The return roller and top of the suspension bracket are seen here from the rear. Various casting seams are visible on the bracket.

The front right sprocket hub and the inside of the sprockets are painted olive drab, as seen in this view. The only spots of bare metal are the teeth of the sprockets where the end connectors make contact.

The upper front side of one of the suspension brackets, or frames, on the right side of the M3 is seen here. The top of a volute spring is at the bottom of the photo, and the track return roller is on top of the bracket. Twisted wires are connected to the hex bolts that attach the frame to the hull.

The rear part of the final drive and several of the hex bolts that secure that unit to the final drive housing are visible on the right front drive-sprocket assembly.

17

The drive sprocket hub was a hollow steel casting to which the sprockets were bolted. Sprockets could thus be removed, reversed, and reinstalled to even out wear on the teeth.

This Lee was used for crew training at Bovington, Dorset soon after the type's adoption by Great Britain in 1941.

The right tail light assembly and electrical cable are seen mounted to the side of the overhang at the rear of the hull. Its light elements (not visible from this side angle) comprise a blackout stop light at top and a blackout light at the bottom.

This pistol port is on the crew compartment's right side. The splash guard's welded bead around the port opening was roughly applied on this M3. The external aperture for the protectoscope is rounded rather than angular.

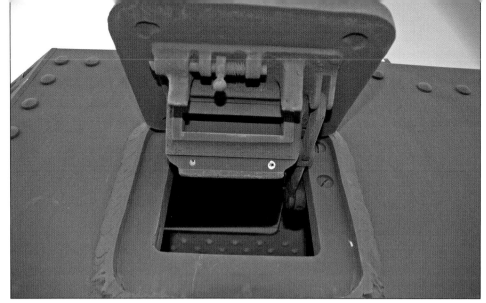

The protectoscope mount on the interior of the pistol port is displayed in this view from below. A viewing prism was fitted into the rectangular aperture in the device. To the right is the hold-open arm, the positioning of which required that the protectoscope be positioned off center on the port. The mechanism with the spring and rounded knob toward the bottom of the protectoscope is the latch that locks the pistol port when closed

The open pistol port on the right side of the hull is seen here looking down from atop the roof of the crew compartment. The joint of the roof and the 1.5-inch-thick side armor plate is visible. The opening for the protectoscope in the pistol port is offset slightly to the side, to accommodate the hold-open arm.

The bearing surface of the barrel of the M3 75mm gun on M3 medium tanks was left as unpainted, smooth metal for about half of the length of the tube, including several inches to the front of the elevating shield assembly (the semi-disc-shaped shield which, in turn, fits into the horizontal rotor shield, the traversing element of the two-part shield arrangement). The tolerances required for the recoil action precluded the use of paint in this area.

Attached to the right fender to the front of the 75mm gun sponson are storage brackets for a bolt cutter, with loops for hold-down straps (not installed here). The boxy object in the foreground and the clips on the fender toward the siren are mounting brackets for a mattock head. The right service headlight and blackout lamp are to the right, and above the siren is the side of the grouser box.

The right service headlight, blackout lamp, and brush guard, including the electrical wiring are seen here from the right side of the vehicle.

The left sealed-beam service headlight, seen here from the front, is a 40-candlepower unit, while the blackout lamp is 3-candlepower. To the left is one of two apertures for fixed .30-caliber machine guns that were intended to be mounted in the hull but were seldom used in service.

Electrical wires are routed from the interior of the hull, through a T-fitting, to the right headlight group, seen here from the front under the brush guard and adjacent to the siren.

The driver turned on the siren, seen here adjacent to the right headlight, by pushing a button next to his left foot. Knurled, threaded collars secure the electrical cables to the T-fitting, which, in turn, is fitted to the fender.

Only the rear-most bogie bracket on the right suspension of this M3 vehicle features horizontal ribs.

In this frontal view of the late-production Chrysler M3 belonging to the National Museum of Americans in Wartime, casting numbers are visible on the transmission cover: 100 on the right section (to the left in the photo), and A107 on the left section.

The part number E1230 appears on the side of the right final drive housing. Next to the number is a G in an octagon, the foundry symbol for American Steel Foundries' plant in Granite City, Illinois. Around and below the fill plug for the final drive is spilled engine oil, the lubricant for that unit.

The left final drive housing bears the part number E1231 and the symbol of American Steel Foundries' Granite City, Illinois, plant, followed by a 1. The locking nuts used in combination with hex bolts to join together the sections of the transmission housing are visible here, as is the left towing eye, which is an integral part of the casting.

This is a frontal view of the 75mm main gun's elevation shield (through with the gun barrel passes) and rotor shield. Note the beveled edge around the opening of the rotor shield through which the elevation shield projects.

This is a close-up of the casting that contains the apertures for two fixed .30-caliber machine guns in the bow. Hex bolts set into spotfaces attach the transmission housing to the glacis underneath that casting.

The contours of the the .30-caliber machine gun apertures are visible in this view from directly overhead.

Plugs have been welded into this pair of .30-caliber apertures to seal out the elements and projectile splash.

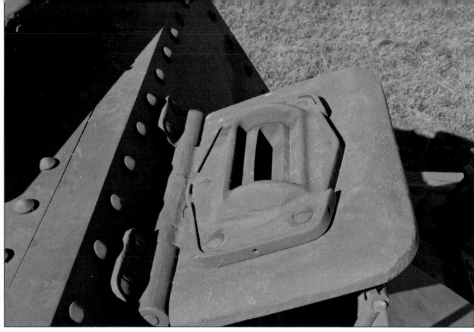

In this view through the driver's open vision port, the protectoscope assembly is visible, along with the sprung latch that locks the port when closed. The lower end of the hold-open arm of the port attaches to a bracket on the glacis.

This is the outside of the driver's vision port, showing the slotted, oval-headed screws that secure the protectoscope to the port. One end of the hinge pin is visible at the bottom of the photo.

Engine Data

Engine Make/Model	Continental R975 EC2	GM 6046	Chrysler A57
Number of Cylinders	9	2x6	30
Cubic Inch Displacement	973	850	1,253
Horsepower	340@2,400 rpm	410@2,100 rpm	425@2,400 rpm
Torque	890@1,800 rpm	885@1,900 rpm	1,060@1,800 rpm

Lee Techincal Data

Model	M3	M3A1	M3A2	M3A3	M3A4	M3A5
Max Speed	24	24	24	25	20	25
Fuel Capacity	175	175	175	148	160	148
Range	120	120	120	150	100	150
Electrical	24 Neg	24 Neg	24 Neg	24 Neg	24 Neg	24 Neg
Transmission Speeds	5F 1R	5F 1R	5F 1R	5F 1R	5F 1R	5F 1R

Lee General Data

Model	M3	M3A1	M3A2	M3A3	M3A4	M3A5
Weight^	61,500	63,000	60,400	63,000	64,000	64,000
Length*	222	222	222	222	242	222
Width*	107	107	107	107	104	107
Height*	123	123	123	123	123	123
Tread	83	83	83	83	83	83
Crew	6 or 7	6 or 7	6 or 7	6 or 7	6 or 7	6 or 7
Turning Radius (Feet)	31	31	31	31	35	31
Armament Main Secondary Flexible	75mm 37mm 3x.30	75mm 37mm 3x.30	75mm 37mm 3x.30	75 mm 37mm 3x.30	75mm 37mm 3x.30	75mm 37mm 3x.30

^Fighting Weight
*Overall dimensions listed in inches.

This round casting forms part of the roof over the sponson-mounted 75mm gun, and also incorporates a bearing for the top trunnion of the traverse shield below the screwed-on circular plate at the center of the casting. Also on the casting is the housing for the gunner's M1 periscope. The housing rotates in unison with the traverse of the gun, and the periscope elevates in unison with the gun. Casting numbers can be seen on several of the roof plates.

The roof over the sponson gun appears to the right of the turret. Roof stiffeners reinforce the hull. A capital S inside a diamond, the foundry mark of the Sivyer Steel Casting Company, is visible on the large circular plate. Small studs are installed around the perimeter of the gunner's periscope mount for attaching a canvas periscope cover. A splash guard partly encircles the travel area of the periscope mount.

The left fender, lights, and, at the bottom right, the .30-caliber machine gun port are visible from the roof of the M3.

The gunner's periscope mount features openings at the front and rear. Protective guards flank the housing on both sides. On the roof to the left of the sponson is a track grouser stowage box.

The barrel of the M3's main gun appears on the left side of this photograph, shot from atop the sponson roof. Below and to the right of the gun barrel, mounted atop the right fender, are the headlight, blackout marker, brush guard, and, at the bottom left, the siren.

This is a head-on view from the front of the tank of the roof over the sponson gun mount. Slotted, oval-head screws secure the circular plate to the top of the casting at the front of the mount. Behind that plate are the roof hatch and ventilator with a tall splash guard. Looking towards the inboard side of the front of the sponson roof, it is evident that the top edge of the front casting of the sponson has been cut down slightly, and the edge of the circular plate adjoining it has been beveled downward, to allow the gunner's periscope a somewhat improved downward field of vision.

The cam latch and handle and their mounting flange, which is secured to the hatch with two rivets, are visible in this view of the inside of the open roof hatch. The edge of the hatch is recessed to fit the opening in the roof. Also, the thickness of the half-inch roof armor is visible.

On the right side of the M3, roof hatch and ventilator can be seen. The two rivets toward the front end of the hatch are fasteners for a cam latch on the interior of the hatch. Screws are used instead of rivets at the rear of the roof because the left rear of the plate (the top edge of which is next to the row of screws) was designed to be detachable to facilitate removal of the 75mm main gun from the tank.

The ventilator and splash guard and roof hatch are seen here from the rear deck of the M3. The two openings at the rear of the splash guard were designed to drain any water that might get in. A neat welding bead attaches the splash guard to the roof. Below the pistol port on the turret is the foundry mark, a capital H within a C, signifying that the turret was cast by the Continental Foundry and Machine Company in East Chicago, Indiana.

The top of the ventilator and splash guard at the right rear of the crew compartment roof are seen here. To the top left of the photo, on the rear deck, is the armored cover for the right sponson fuel tank.

In this view, looking down from atop the turret, the 37mm gun barrel at left partially obscures the ventilator and splash guard at the front left corner of the roof over the crew compartment. At the center is a stowage box. The front end of the splash guard surrounding the turret is visible between the turret and the roof stiffener at the bottom left of the photo.

This is a view of the right side of the roof of a different, ex-Commonwealth M3. Below the pistol port on the turret is the foundry mark of the letter C within an octagon, the symbol for ASF's East Chicago, Indiana, Cast Armor Plant. On this example, a splash guard was tack welded to the roof around the perimeter of the turret, a feature not seen on all M3s.

A periscope mount with a built-in guard was mounted on the roof over the driver's position on this ex-Commonwealth M3 (the open driver's hatch is to the far left). Also visible are the remnants of the center stowage box, which was removed with a torch when the periscope was added.

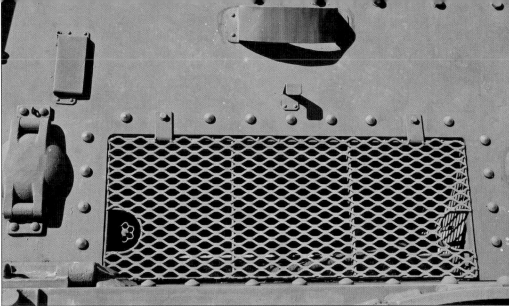

The rear deck and storage boxes are seen on this M3 in the collection of the National Museum of Americans in Wartime. At the center of the deck are brackets for a shovel. Clips for storing a tow cable are arranged around the deck. To remove the two engine compartment access plates, it is necessary to remove the many hex bolts around their perimeters.

Brackets fixed to the top of the right storage box lid were intended to hold the manual engine starting crank.

Hex bolts in two flanges at the rear of the engine air inlet grille secure it to the deck. Below the semicircular cutouts on each side of the grille are shutoff valves for the two inner fuel tanks. The knurled control knob is attached to one valve, missing on the other.

An idler adjustment wrench was normally stored on the lid of the left storage box, seen here from the center of the rear deck. The serrated, faucet-type knob visible through the round cutout in the forward engine compartment cover controls a fuel shutoff valve for the left sponson fuel tank. This arrangement is mirrored for the right side tank.

These are the details of the forward right part of the front engine compartment cover, with the engine air intake grille centered at the front of the plate and the rear of the crew compartment, which is at the top of the photograph. The knob for the fuel shutoff valve for the right sponson fuel tank is visible in the cutout in the plate near the storage box at the lower right.

Embossed on top of each of the fire extinguisher housings are the words: "KIDDE LUX / FIRE EXTINGUISHING SYSTEM / WALTER KIDDE & COMPANY, INC. / BLOOMFIELD, NEW JERSEY / MADE IN U.S.A. PAT PENDING."

On the left side of the forward cover of the engine compartment are three fuel filler covers (including the one for the auxiliary generator tank below the antenna bracket at the upper left). Slots in the bottom of the antenna bracket allowed water to run out. On the rear wall of the crew compartment, to the right of the antenna bracket, are the housings for the two external actuating handles for the internal fire extinguisher system.

The antenna bracket of the M3 contained a sprung antenna mount. This splash guard around the turret, consisting of sections of curved steel bars intermittently-welded to the hull roof, was added to many vehicles while in Australian service.

This view is looking down the barrel of the turret-mounted M6 37mm cannon. The combination gun mount was designated the M24, and also included an M1919A4 .30-caliber machine gun (not installed here). The shield of the M24 mount is fastened to the front of the turret with slotted, oval-head screws. On the face of the M24's shield, below the aperture for the gunner's M2 periscopic sight, are casting numbers and the foundry mark of the Continental Foundry and Machine Company, Coraopolis, Pennsylvania (a capital D inscribed in a C).

A wider view of the top of the turret and gun, with the edge of the cupola at bottom left, part of the 75mm gunner's periscope mount to the right, and the open driver's front vision port at the upper right.

The barrel of the 37mm gun passes through the rotor shield, as seen in this view from above. The hole on the shield to the right of the barrel accommodated an M1919A4 .30-caliber coaxial machine gun (not installed). To the bottom center is the rooftop stowage box, and the open driver's side vision port.

The foundry mark on the roof of the turret identifies the manufacturer of the turret as the Continental Foundry and Machine Company's plant in East Chicago, Indiana. (The H stood for the plant's original name, Hubbard Steel Foundry.) The casting number on the roof is 7216 1309 D38530. (The 1309 is lightly stamped on a slightly raised, oblong projection.) Special armored oval countersunk screws hold the mantlet securely to the turret casting.

This is a close-up of the aperture in the M24 gun mount's shield for the 37mm gunner's periscope. An illegible number is stamped in the roughly molded, oblong "placard" below the foundry mark.

This is a side view of the M24 gun mount's shield and the front, right facet of the turret, complete with gouges and scars. The cylinder below the barrel is a counterweight required to balance the gun for purposes of the gyrostabilizer.

A canvas dust cover is draped over the M6 37mm gun and shield of this ex-Commonwealth M3. Stenciled in black toward the top of it is identifying information, including the part number, D51353. Grommets are arranged around the edges of the cover for securing it to studs, not installed on this gun shield. Note the zippered flap that can be rolled up and secured to allow viewing through the periscope.

This side view of the 37mm mount from a higher angle shows the casting numbers and foundry mark on the turret roof and the upper surfaces of the 37mm gun's rotor shield and periscope rotor. The M2 periscopic sight was at the gunner's eye level and comprised an "observing" element on the left side and a telescopic element for targeting on the right side.

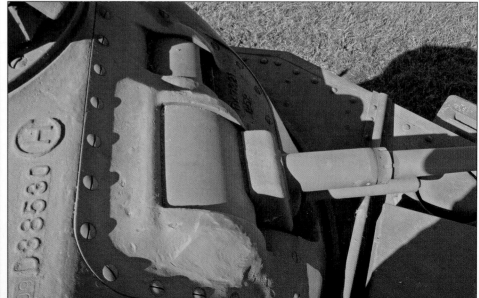

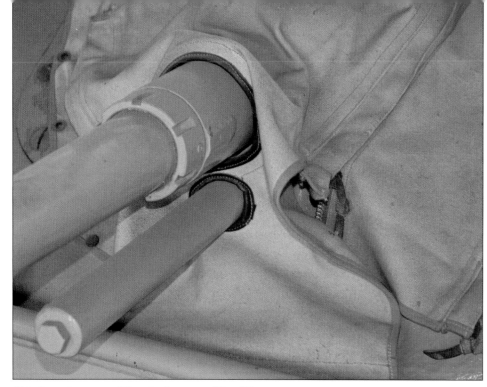

This is a close-up of the dust cover of the 37mm gun.

This is the rear of the turret of the M3, with the cupola on top of it. The cupola is turned to the side, with the front to the left. The cupola's M1919A4 .30-caliber machine gun is not installed. The pistol port is to the right of the turret, with the pistol port at the rear of the crew compartment below it. The rear part of the splash guard surrounding the bottom of the turret is also visible.

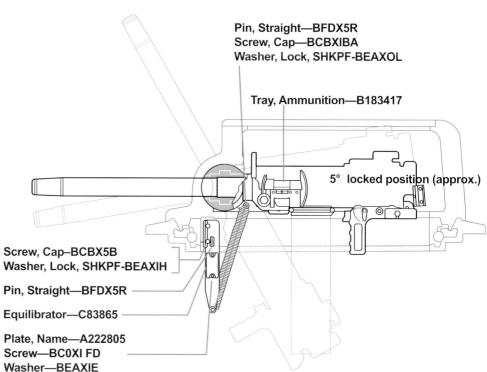

Pin, Straight—BFDX5R
Screw, Cap—BCBXIBA
Washer, Lock, SHKPF-BEAXOL

Tray, Ammunition—B183417

5° locked position (approx.)

Screw, Cap—BCBX5B
Washer, Lock, SHKPF-BEAXIH

Pin, Straight—BFDX5R

Equilibrator—C83865

Plate, Name—A222805
Screw—BC0XI FD
Washer—BEAXIE

This drawing illustrates the cupola-mounted machine gun's range of elevation. The hand grip's configuration (hand grip is mounted on the underside of the machine gun receiver) is unique to this application. A conventional, rear-mounted grip and trigger would have been awkward to use and would have cramped the cupola so as to render it unusable.

A close-up shows the loader's pistol port (right side of the turret), equipped with a protectoscope. Note the contours of the swell at the top of the turret to accommodate the cupola.

The rear left side of the turret and the front of the cupola appear here. The vehicle commander was stationed at or within the cupola and controlled a .30-caliber machine gun that projected through the rotor to the right of the cupola (to the left in this photo). In the other rotor to the right of the machine gun was a protectoscope. Open here are the two direct vision ports with hinged, armored covers on the side of the cupola.

The front left side of the cupola is viewed here from below. The curved brackets at either side of the top front of the cupola support the bi-folding hatch when open.

The hinged, armored cover of the left direct vision port is open, showing a metal cover with four very thin vision slits fastened over the port. The ring-shaped object toward the front of the cupola is the trunnion of the machine gun and the sight rotor.

At the rear of the cupola is the foundry mark for the Continental Foundry and Machine Company's plant in East Chicago, Indiana. In the foreground is the turret roof ventilator, surrounded by a substantial splash guard.

The split hatch at the top of the cupola is bi-folding, with four external hinges. In the forward section of the hatch is a small, circular port for signaling with flags. Arranged around the hatch at the top of the cupola are three threaded sockets for inserting lifting eyes when it was necessary to remove the cupola.

The ventilator bears the foundry mark of an S within a diamond, indicating it was cast by the Sivyer Steel Casting Company. The three slotted, oval-headed screws to the front of the ventilator protrude down into the ceiling inside the turret to secure the top of the cylinder of the 37mm gun stabilizer system.

When the lifting eyes weren't in use, hex bolts were placed in the sockets as plugs; only most distant of the sockets has a hex bolt in it in this view of the right side of the cupola.

Seen here from the front of the turret, four viewing slits are visible in this close-up view of the A213101 protector fastened in the cupola's direct vision port with four slotted screws. To the right in the picture is the right-hand trunnion of the machine gun and sight rotor. The side of the right hatch support is visible on the top of the front of the cupola.

Large, slotted, oval-head screws secure the cupola ring, seen here from the left, to the roof of the turret. Note the two relief holes at the rear of the ventilator splash guard, to let out any water that falls into it.

The casting numbers and foundry mark on the front of the turret roof stand out in this close-up view.

This is a close-up of the turret ventilator and surrounding splash guard.

The loader's pistol port on the right side of the turret, the front-rear roof stiffener, and the ventilator and splash guard at the right rear of the crew compartment roof are seen here. To the upper left is the engine air intake grille on the rear deck. A splash guard surrounds the base of the turret

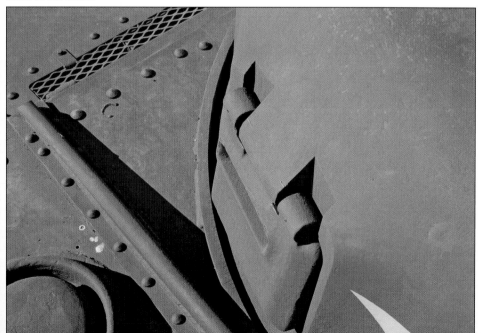

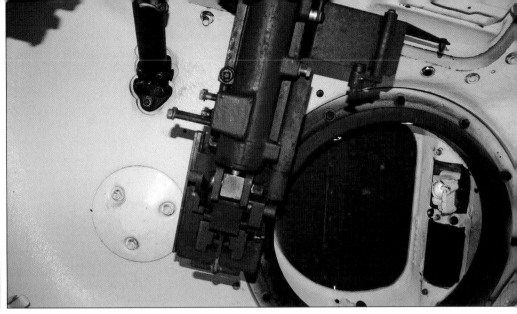

A view through the cupola hatch down into the turret and turret basket of an M3. At the bottom of the photo is the gunner's seat, to the rear of which is a height-adjustable, folding seat on the turret basket. This seat doubled as a platform for the commander to stand on when standing up through the cupola hatch. At the right is a folding seat for the commander, mounted on the side of the turret. On the side of the recoil guard for the M6 37mm gun at the left are a nomenclature plate and casting number. Ready racks for 37mm ammunition are arranged at various places on the turret and basket.

In this view from the bottom of the turret basket, details of the underside of the 37mm gun are evident. The fixture attached to the ceiling next to the gun is the cylinder of the gyrostabilizer system. The circular plate is the ventilator. The cupola interior is visible on the other side of the gun; note the olive drab hatch, the .30-caliber machine gun mount, and sighting periscope mount. The m.g. mount and periscope elevated or depressed in unison, and the machine gun mount also had a swivel for traversing right or left without rotating the entire cupola.

The recoil shield of the 37mm gun is to the left of the gun itself. The black nomenclature plate identifies it as the "MOUNT, COMBINATION / GUN, M24" manufactured by Chrysler Corporation in 1942. Below the casting number on the guard is the foundry mark of Unitcast Corp., Toledo, Ohio. To the left is the tray for the ammunition box for the coaxial .30-caliber machine gun, with the guide track for the ammunition belt visible over the 37mm gun barrel. Below the tray is the rotor shield and below that is the elevation handwheel.

The recoil guard has been removed from the M24 combination gun mount in this photo of the underside of the 37mm gun. The rotor guard, next to the elevation hand wheel at the edge of the photo, is painted white on the sides and olive drab on the surface that would be exposed on the outside of the turret when the gun is raised to maximum elevation. The .37mm gun and the .30-caliber ammunition tray are also olive drab. Note the elevation gear next to the rotor guard and the ready racks for 37mm ammunition on the turret wall.

The right side of the turret and turret basket are viewed here from below the 37mm gun. The elevating gear is to the upper left. The loader's pistol port is near the center of the photo. It has the protectoscope holder but no viewing prism. The locking latch at the bottom of the port and the operating lever to the left of the port are missing.

A view toward the front left corner of the driver's compartment, with the exterior of the turret basket to the left. The driver's side and front vision ports are open. Projecting at the center, below the instrument panel, is the cradle for the fixed, twin .30-caliber machine guns that could be mounted to fire through the bow. The cradle is supported by an adjustable post so that the elevation of the guns could be varied. The elevating wheel of the sponson-mounted 75mm gun is to the far right.

The controls in front of the gunner's seat include, left to right, the hydraulic traverse gearbox (with clutch lever and manual control lever to the right of it); the aluminum-colored, pistol grip–type hydraulic traverse control handle, including electrically powered triggers for the 37mm and .30-caliber guns; and the elevation hand wheel. Provisions were made for traversing the turret by hydraulic or manual power. The drive cogwheel at the bottom of the traverse gearbox engages the ring gear of the turret through a small cutout in the turret basket.

The driver's and sponson gunner's area is seen here through the front opening of the turret basket. The hydraulic traverse control handle is at the upper left, with the elevation hand wheel to the upper center.

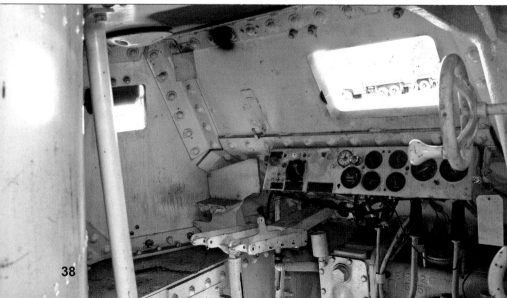

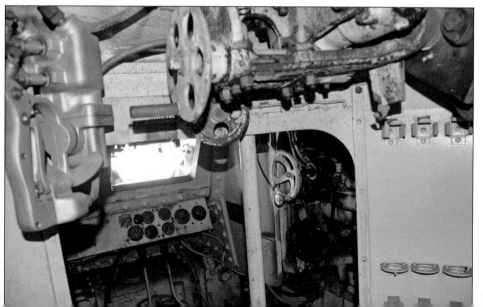

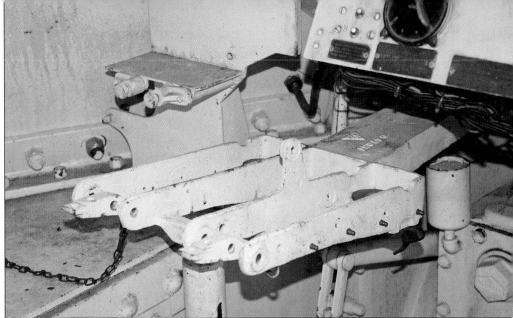

Mounted on the left wall to the front of the turret is a 37mm ammunition box. The abbreviations stand for armor piercing, high explosive, and canister. The post in the foreground supports the roof to the front of the turret. Next to the open vision port is the operating lever. The dark red splotches are spot primer.

On the left of the instrument panel is the starter switch. Instruments shown on the panel include (top row, from left) a clock, fuel primer, oil temperature gauge, oil pressure gauge; (bottom row, from left) engine-hour meter, voltmeter, and ammeter; and speedometer to the right. The weld beads around the rivet heads above the instrument panel were an extra measure to prevent hits by incoming projectiles from sending the rivets ricocheting around the compartment.

This close-up shows the cradle for the twin fixed .30-caliber machine guns, with the top of the support post below the rear of it. The cylinder to the right of the cradle is the breather for the left steering brake housing.

The driver's seat, minus its cushion and backrest, is seen here near the center of the photograph, with the gunner's seat to the right and the front of the vehicle to the top right. The driver's seat straddles the transmission, with curved steering/brake levers on either side of the transmission. The triangular bracket at the rear of the seat is the attachment point for a two-piece seatbelt. The clutch pedal is visible to the left of the left lever. To the lower left are stowage boxes, including one for fourteen 250-round belts of .30-caliber ammunition at the far left.

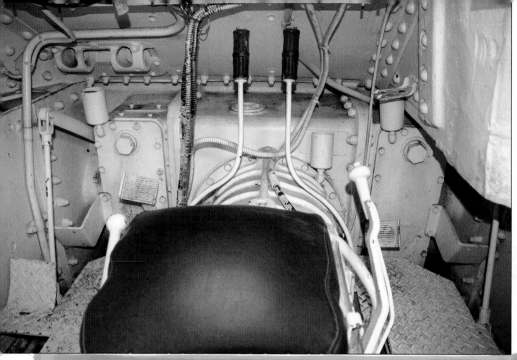

The transmission and the steering/brake levers are seen from the driver's vantage point in a tank with an intact seat. To the right of the right lever is the transmission breather.

The recoil system on this side view of the M3 75mm gun is painted white and includes top and bottom recoil cylinders. The dark-colored cylinder is the breech-closing spring, which operates a roller chain that closes the breech. The operating handle is not installed in the large aperture on the chain terminal crank's side, just behind the breech-closing spring. The firing solenoid is the small white cylinder below and behind the elevation wheel, and to the rear of it is the firing lever link. The link that synchronizes the gun elevation with the angle of elevation of the M1 periscope is behind the elevation wheel.

The 75mm gunner's seat with a fold-down backrest is viewed from behind. The seat is mounted on a support that is attached to the gun cradle so the gunner could move in unison with the gun as he traversed it. To the left of this position is the driver's seat. The metal panel featuring a diamond tread pattern at the bottom of the photo covers a box containing 35 rounds of 75mm ammunition.

In this view of the gunner's controls, the top hand wheel controls the 75mm gun's elevation. Immediately above the gearbox of the wheel is the mount for the gunner's M1 periscope. The lower wheel is the traverse hand wheel. To the right is the breech of the M3 75mm cannon.

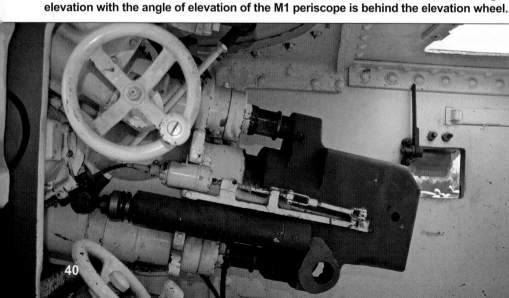

Stabilization system elements are in the front of the sponson to the right of the gun, the breech and top recoil cylinder of which are at far left. The 75mm gun stabilizer system worked to keep the gun's elevation on target even as the tank pitched while moving. At the top is the oil reservoir, with the Westinghouse motor and pump unit to the right of it. Farther forward and partially visible is the cylinder.

The locking latch at the bottom of the door of the rear pistol port is intact, as is part of the opener mechanism to the top right of the door, but several parts, including the operating lever and the retainer for the protectoscope viewing prism, are missing on this vehicle.

The rear pistol port is partially visible to the left of the turret basket (far right) in the right rear corner of the crew compartment of the late-production Chrysler M3, behind the 75mm gun. On the ceiling is a ventilator. The vertical plate behind the ceiling ventilator was meant to be removable and is secured with nuts and bolts instead of rivets.

The slatted fixture at the lower right of this photo of the right rear of the crew compartment is the oil cooler for the engine, with part of the oil tank visible at the bottom center of the photo. At the lower right is the drive (or propeller) shaft where it enters the crew compartment from the engine compartment. At the top right is a row of upper storage clips for 37mm ammunition; the lower row of clips has been removed.

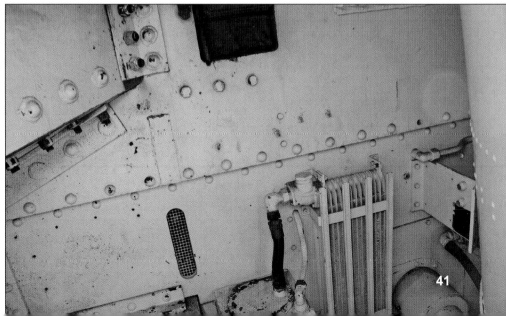

41

Late-production M3s without side doors had an escape hatch in the floor toward the right rear of the crew compartment. It has two lifting handles and four locking bolts operated from a central handle on a rotary mechanism. The oil cooler and tank at the rear of the compartment are to the left, with the dark-colored oil filler cap on top of the lower extension of the tank. The rear of the 75mm ammunition box is to the right.

The top of the oil cooler is at the left and the turret basket on the right in this view across the firewall at the rear of the crew compartment.

Retainer clips protrude in groups of four from the rear of the storage box designed to hold 35 rounds of 75mm ammunition and located to the rear of the 75mm gunner's seat.

Mounted on the turret floor of the M3 to the rear of the 37mm gunner's seat is a Pincor compound motor, which powered the hydraulic systems of the turret. The pump motor and hydraulic lines are to the right. Visible through the opening in the turret basket is the auxiliary power unit in the left rear of the crew compartment.

42

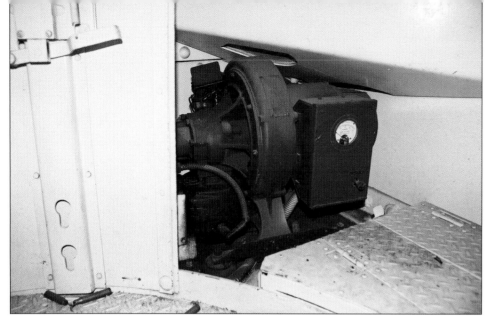

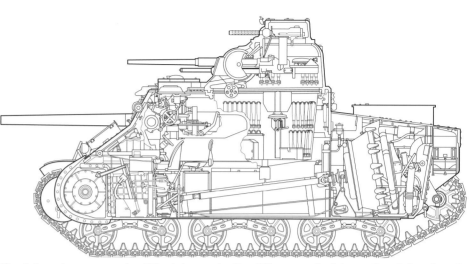

The auxiliary power unit is partially visible through the opening in the turret basket. To the right is the control box, with an ammeter and starter button on the front, and to the left is the flywheel motor and fan housing. Out of view to the left are the magneto shield and a heating duct. The APU was used to preheat the engine in cold weather, charge the batteries, and heat the fighting compartment.

Key internal components of the late-production M3 appear in this sectional drawing. At the rear, the nine-cylinder radial engine is positioned at an angle, with the drive shaft proceeding at the same angle below the turret basket to the transmission. The front of the turret basket is illustrated in exploded-view format to show the 75mm gun's breech and recoil shield. Stored 37mm rounds are shown in the turret and turret basket.

A technical drawing portrays the left side of a late-production M3 with the long 75mm main gun and side doors still present.

The maximum elevations of the three gun mounts of the M3A1 are emphasized in this technical drawing.

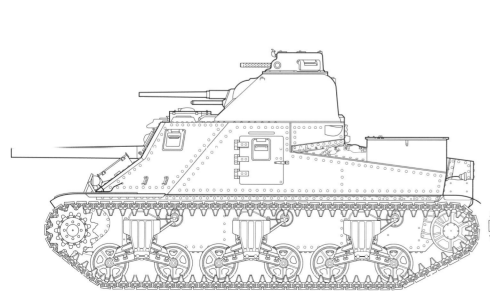

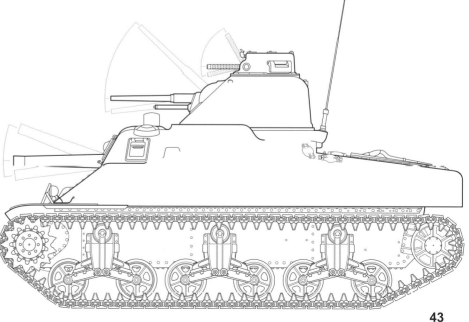

The M3A1 medium tank was essentially the M3 medium tank with a cast hull. American Locomotive Company manufactured three hundred of them from February 1942 to July 1942. This preserved example at Aberdeen Proving Ground, dubbed "Lu Lu Belle," is actually serial number 1962. Its original registration number was W-306032.

In this close-up of the left sprocket and part of the forward bogie, the support arm of the road wheel is at an abnormally compressed angle. It would normally be at a more downward angle while on a flat surface. The lower hull is of riveted construction.

The one-piece upper hull casting gave the M3A1 a combat-loaded weight of 1,500 pounds more than the M3, but it took fewer man-hours to manufacture, was ballistically stronger than riveted plates, and eliminated the danger of rivets popping off and ricocheting around the interior of the vehicle when struck by projectiles. Note the rounded shape of the side door as compared to the squared door of the M3.

Casting numbers and a foundry mark on the hub cap can be seen in this view of the left idler assembly and the track end connectors.

The track return rollers on this vehicle have been raised several inches over the normal height by installing spacers on top of the roller supports, as can be seen in this view of the left rear bogie assembly. As a result, there is a slight upswing of the tracks over the bogies, as opposed to the nearly flat span of the upper run of tracks when the lower rollers were installed. The 20-9 rubber tires are cracked and deteriorating, and the tire is completely missing on the rear road wheel of the center bogie (left).

The driver's forward and side vision ports on the M3A1 were similar to those of the M3. A roof ventilator with splash guard, a later retrofit to this particular vehicle, is next to the side port. The textures on the cast surface of the upper hull range from smooth to pitted. Various grinding marks are visible, and there is a flattened area next to the U below the side vision port.

The side doors of the M3A1 are equipped with pistol ports fitted with protectoscopes. A splash guard surrounds the door, and a grab bar is welded above the top of it. Some late-production M3A1s eliminated the side doors, retaining only one pistol port on the right side of the hull.

The two holes at the bottom of the splash guard around the ventilator on the roof were designed to let out any water that collects inside. The side vision port has been fitted with a protectoscope.

There area bowl-shaped antenna brackets on each side of the hull at the rear of the crew compartment. Housings for the actuating handles for the interior fixed fire extinguishers are to the right of the left antenna bracket. The housings are skewed to the sides (normally the tops were level with each other), and the handles are lying on the hull. The armored fuel-filler covers are for, left to right, the auxiliary power unit fuel tank, left sponson tank, and left inboard tank.

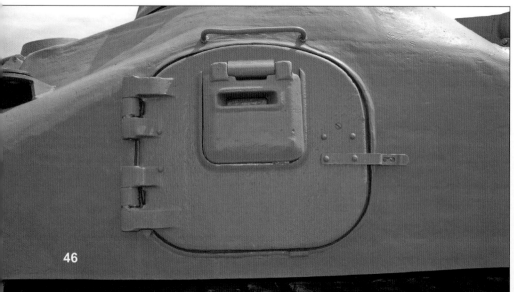

Below the upper hull, the rear of the M3A1 resembles that of late-production M3s, with twin doors for the engine compartment, boxy oil-bath air cleaners on either side, and outlets for the fishtail-type exhausts over the doors. Slight protrusions cast into the rear overhang of the upper hull accommodated the tops of the original "pepper pot" exhausts. Tail lights are mounted flush in the overhang. The badly damaged mud guards, made of thick rubber painted olive drab, rest on the T48 tracks with rubber chevrons.

To the right of the right air cleaner is the remnant of the mud guard. The texture of the casting on the hull can be seen on the overhang at the top of the photo.

The left idler wheel rests on the collar of the spindle housing. The free end of the spring locking clip on top of the housing near the large track-adjusting nut must be unlocked and slid toward the center of the vehicle in order to adjust track tension. There is a triangular door stop located above the lower hinge of the engine compartment door towards the top right of the picture.

The left oil-bath air cleaner lacks several of the retaining rods and wing nuts that hold the oil cup at the bottom in place. The oil-bath cleaner is mounted by a flange on its side to the armor plate next to it, using nuts and bolts.

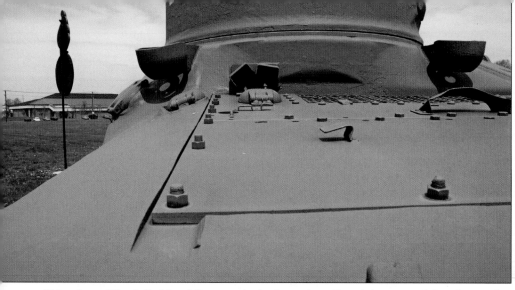

This view of the left side of the rear deck shows how the plates comprising the engine compartment cover are secured with nuts tightened onto threaded studs. To the right is a bracket for a shovel; to the front of it is the engine air intake grille.

The pistol port at the rear of the right side of the crew compartment of the M3 was not carried over to the M3A1, but the roof hatch was included, although repositioned and at an angle to the centerline of the tank. This tank has the early-production arrangement with the hinge toward the front. As this arrangement made it awkward to open the hatch, the hinge was moved to the rear of the hatch on later M3A1s. Note on the hatch the casting number and the capital U within a keystone: the foundry mark of Union Steel Castings.

This side view of the M3A1's idler spindle housing also shows that the side and rear retaining rods are installed on the right air cleaner.

The arrangement of the roof hatch and right side door can be seen on this right side view of Lu Lu Belle.

Details of the sponson casting, the elevation and horizontal rotor shields, and the manner in which the fender is bolted to the sponson are visible in this view of the M2 75mm gun. On the fender are brackets for a mattock head and a machine gun tripod. A canvas dust cover can be snapped on the studs surrounding the rotor shield.

A casting line is faintly visible on the vertical centerline of the elevation rotor shield in this head-on view of the sponson gun mount. The service headlight and blackout marker lamp have been removed from the vehicle, but their mounting bracket and brush guard remain in place.

50

Various textures are visible on the irregular and slightly wavy surface of the upper hull casting. There are Y-shaped spacers at the top of the roller supports on the bogie frames, which raise the track return rollers several inches.

The top of the 75mm sponson mount and the left side of the roof of the M3A1 appear in this photograph. The round rotor cover and the periscope housing both bear the foundry marks of Symington-Gould. The small studs that surround the perimeter of the splash guard around the periscope mount are intended to facilitate attachment of a canvas periscope cover. The ventilator and splash guard visible in this view were later retrofits to this particular vehicle.

The ports for the two fixed .30-caliber machine guns are in a swelling at the left front corner of the upper hull casting. The left service headlight and blackout marker lamp have been removed, and a later blackout headlight and brush guard, atypical for the M3A1, have been installed over the gun ports. Hex bolts attach the top of the three-piece transmission/differential cover.

The hinge and top of the driver's forward vision port, along with the roof ventilator and splash guard, are seen here from the front of the M3A1. Slotted, oval-head screws attach the protectoscope housing to the forward vision port. The S-in-a-circle foundry mark of Symington-Gould Corporation is on the top of the protectoscope housing.

Details of the rear hatch, with its hinge and the Union Steel Castings foundry mark, are apparent in this view, as are features on the rear deck. Those include clips for storing a shovel and axe, and armored covers for the filler caps of the right inboard and right fuel tanks. The loader's pistol port, located on the right side of the turret, is visible to the upper right.

On the right side of the turret is the loader's pistol port, equipped with a protectoscope. The surface of the turret is mostly pitted, but there are also some smooth areas, such as around the pistol port hinge.

The gun seen on the front right side of the cupola of the M3A1 appears to be an M5 37mm cannon, as indicated by the absence below the gun tube of the characteristic counterweight used on the M6 gun. Not installed on this vehicle are the M1919A4 .30-caliber machine guns in the M24 coaxial mount and its cupola.

Hold-open brackets for the bi-folding hatch are bolted to the top front of the cupola. The cupola features complex contours on the casting and flat, milled surfaces on the face of the direct vision slot cover and the top of the 37mm shield. A casting number is on the beveled top surface of the vision slot cover.

One solid, stamped road wheel, uncommon on M3s, is in the rear position on the front bogie of this M3A1 at Aberdeen Proving Ground. The other wheels are of the more typical, open-spoked type. Like the front road wheel and suspension arm on the left side of this vehicle, the right front wheel and arm are at an unusually high attitude, with the arm almost parallel to the ground. The 75mm gun is the short, M2 version. It lacks the counterweight at the end that was installed when the gun was equipped with a gyrostabilizer system.

Baldwin Locomotive Works manufactured 322 M3A3s with welded hulls and a General Motors Model 6046 diesel engine that consisted of two GM Detroit Diesel 6-71 six-cylinder engines with their outputs linked to a common collector gear. This variant was designated the Lee V when used by Commonwealth forces. U.S. use of the diesel-powered Lee seems to have been confined to training purposes. The M3A5 was similar to the M3A3, but featured a riveted rather than a welded hull. (Patton Museum)

The factory producing this vehicle welded shut the left side door and pistol port and plugged the protectoscope port.

This photo of the left front of the upper hull of an M3A3 shows the welded hull plates and the welded-shut side door with its pistol port. Grouser boxes are welded to the glacis and the roof over the driver's compartment. The two brackets below the painted letter L were designed for storage of a machine gun tripod.

The welded plates to the rear of the left side of the M3A3's crew compartment are evident in this photo. The steel tow cable is lying on the armored fuel filler covers. At the top is the base of the antenna bracket. The housings of the fixed fire extinguisher handles are painted red.

The welded joints of the rear plates and the extra-tall plate at the rear of the upper hull, intended to protect the radiator, are visible on the left, rear of this M3A3. The wiring for the tail light assembly is also exposed and visible.

This side view shows that the counterweight at the end of the barrel of the M2 75mm gun on the M3A3 medium tank consists of two parts that are bolted together. The longer M3 75mm guns on some of the M3-family medium tanks did not require the counterweight in order for the gun to operate in unison with the gyrostabilizer system.

This file photo of the rear of the pilot M3A3 was taken at Aberdeen Proving Ground on 26 November 1941. The pilot vehicle was the only one of the M3A3s to have riveted hull construction. The somewhat battered structure below the rear plate of the upper hull is a sheet metal exhaust baffle. (Patton Museum)

This view of the underside of the counterweight on the 75mm gun barrel shows the four bolts and nuts and the recesses for them in the casting of the bottom half of the counterweight assembly.

When looking at the controls of the 75mm gun taken from behind the gunner's seat, the elevating hand wheel appears toward the top, seen in profile, and the traversing hand wheel is below, with the firing button for the gun on top of the hub. The bare metal box with two large, black buttons to the front of, and partially blocked by, the gear box of the elevating hand wheel is the control box, with the firing and stabilizer switch box below it. At the top, right is the mount for the M1 periscope, including a head rest. The driver's controls and instrument panel are to the left.

A forward-facing view of the space between the right side of the 75mm gun and the sponson wall. The white cylinder at the upper center of the photo is the gyrostabilizer motor and pump, and the dark-colored mechanism below it is the gyro control box. Beneath the gyro control box is the traversing gear, comprising a rack and pinion. The commemorative plaque below the fire extinguisher gives some of the history of this tank, including the fact that it was transferred to the Brazilian army toward the end of World War II and returned to the United States in 1976.

The Grant cruiser tank was built for use by the British, to their specifications. It was essentially an M3 with a different style of cast turret and a large bustle to accommodate the No. 19 wireless transmitter/receiver. This M3 Grant in a four-color desert camouflage scheme is owned by the National Museum of Americans in Wartime.

The Grant comes to a stop, showing how its sand shields tend to keep churned-up road dust at a minimum. The turret is traversed to the right, offering a view of the bustle.

The left service headlight and blackout marker are seen here from the side, together with their brush guard. Also visible are the braided jackets on the electrical cables for the lights.

The right, side door features a pistol port fitted with a protectoscope. Fixed on the right of the door is a latch for a padlock. The rail below the door was fitted to some Grants as a means for attaching camouflage netting, bedrolls, knapsacks, and other types of gear that might be stored on the vehicle.

As elsewhere on the vehicle, the driver's side vision port featured an opening for a protectoscope indirect vision device. The port hinge is screwed to the hull.

The stowage rail was welded to U-shaped brackets that had been welded to the side of the hull. Other brackets, welded to the outside of the rail at regular intervals, were designed to hold bows, over which a canvas cover could be placed, simulating the cab and cargo area of a tracked carrier vehicle—part of the deception measures the British took preparatory to the Second Battle of El-Alamein in the autumn of 1942.

Grants were outfitted with two types of rear storage box: a tall version, like those used on U.S. M3s on the left, and the much lower type on the right. Both boxes have retainer chains for padlocks (not installed).

Details of the riveted sheet metal construction of the sand shield are visible in this photo. Rather than being welded to the rear deck, the boxes were secured by bent metal straps welded on both of the long sides of the containers.

The Lee was utilized by the First Australian Armoured Division, Second Army Tank Battalion, when the unit was formed late in 1942.

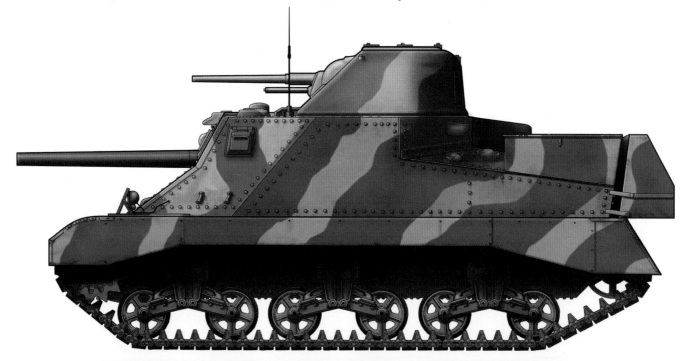

As seen in this left rear three-quarter view, this Grant has the external, box-shaped oil-bath air cleaners on either side of the engine compartment doors. Triangular gusset plates are welded to the bottom of the rear overhang of the upper hull, to the rear of the air cleaners. Some Grants had large, square plates instead of the triangular design.

This Grant has fishtail-type exhaust outlets behind and below both air cleaners. This configuration was a modification effected midway through the M3 production run, and was an improvement over the earlier design, where the exhaust outlets were immediately below the rear hull overhang, frequently resulting in the buildup of hot gases under the overhang.

At the right end of the left idler spindle housing is the idler adjusting nut. A towing clevis is mounted on the left towing eye.

The left exhaust outlet is seen here from the side, with the oil cup and a retaining rod of the left air cleaner to the upper left and the idler adjusting nut below.

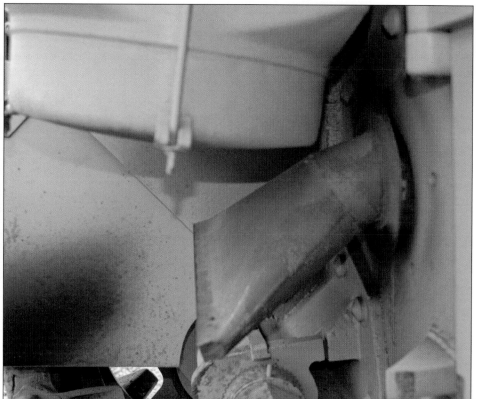

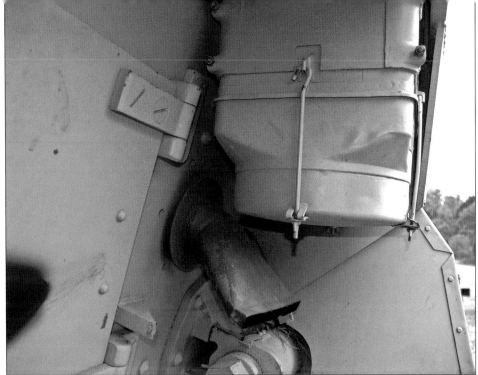

The vehicle's right air cleaner and exhaust are seen here with the engine compartment door to the left. This style of exhaust was introduced about January 1942 to alleviate overheating of the rear engine deck plate caused by the original design.

Data plates on the rear face of both air cleaners and the two antenna mounts on the turret roof can be seen in this view of the right rear of the Grant.

Reinforcements keep the exhaust outlet airflow open. Below it is the right idler's spindle housing. The spring clip on top of it locks in place the collar, which must be unlocked and slid to the left as part of the idler-tensioning process.

This M3 Grant was employed by the British 8th Army in the Middle East during the spring of 1942.

The absence of counterweights on the 37mm and 75mm gun barrels indicates that the guns on this Grant were not gyrostabilized.

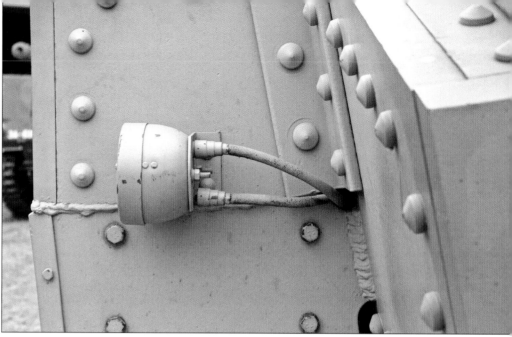

The right taillight assembly and the construction of the side of the rear hull overhang and the rear of the crew compartment (top) are seen here. Two slotted screws hold the cover of the light in place. The word "GUIDE" is stamped below the lower lens. The rivets here have a conical profile.

The lower, right-side storage box is seen here. The right plate of the crew compartment (to the right of the photo) is held in place by slotted screws, rather than rivets, to allow the plate to be taken off for the installation or removal of the 75mm gun.

The taillight housing has a threaded stud at the rear which passes through an L-bracket riveted to the side of the rear hull overhang. A nut tightened on the stud holds the taillight in place. Separate cables provide power to both light elements.

This view of the right, front fender shows the siren, service headlight, blackout marker lamp, and brush guard. To the left are brackets for a mattock head and bolt cutters. The bar welded to the fender at the right is a support for the front end of the stowage rail that runs along the bottom edge of the upper hull.

Different casting marks are on the sides of the right-front bogie suspension arms. The forward suspension arm has a hole for the spacer that ran between the two forward arms. The rear arm is the later version made after the deletion of the spacers.

The sprockets on the vehicle are of the type that was standard on the M3. The bent flanges at the front of the sand shield are shaped to facilitate riveting the sheet metal parts together.

Many of the Eighth British Army Grant tanks were painted in this camouflage pattern by mid-1943.

T-24210

This particular Grant has flat, rectangular sand shields but some Grants had sand shields with curved fronts. With the front vision port open, the driver's face was completely exposed.

This Grant is fitted with WD-212 tracks, a 16-inch double-pin track designed for use on British and Australian Grant and Lee medium tanks. Because of the tread pattern, the track is sometimes called the double-I, double-H, or waffle type.

Details of the lower parts of the flanges of the three-piece transmission/differential/final drive housing are evident, along with the locking nuts that hold them together, in this view of the inner side of the left front suspension.

Commonwealth M3s were fitted with periscope mounts with built-in brush guards installed on the roof over the driver's compartment. In this frontal photo of the Grant, the periscope is to the right of the driver's forward vision port. The twin-.30-caliber fixed machine gun ports have been covered on this tank. The sand shields fit under the stock front fenders. The bars welded to the fender support the front ends of the side stowage rails.

The inner sides of the roadwheels are visible underneath the Grant's hull in this rare view of the vehicle's underside, looking from the front towards the rear.

A bracket, specially designed for the Grant, secures the front of the sand shield to the final drive housing. A flange is welded to the side of the sand shield and fastened with two nuts and bolts to the bracket.

Above the filler plug for the right final drive are casting numbers and the foundry mark of American Steel Foundries' plant in Granite City, Illinois. A pin and cotter pin secure the tow hook on the tow eye.

This wider view of the inner front of the sand shield shows how the shield is tucked under and bolted to the stock M3 fender.

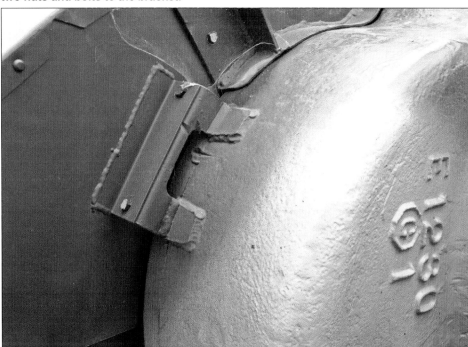

Lubricant stains were almost always found around the filler plugs of the final drives of M3s and Grants. Instead of a tow hook, a tow clevis is attached to the left towing eye of this Grant.

Although some Grants mounted the twin fixed .30-caliber machine guns at the front, the ports on this vehicle have been blanked off, rendering them unusable. The rivets at the top and inboard side of the ports secure the casting to the hull.

The left sand shield is bolted to the a flange that is welded to the left side of the hull of the vehicle.

The casting number and foundry mark of American Steel Foundries' Granite City plant are on the top, left corner of the transmission housing. Hex bolts set into recesses fasten the top of the housing to the front of the upper hull. Part of the fixed machine gun port can be seen at the upper right of the photograph.

The left headlight, blackout lamp, and brush guard, are seen here from the left front of the vehicle. To the far right is the support for the front of the side stowage rail.

The electrical wires for the right headlight, blackout marker, and siren exit the hull through a T-connection near the right headlight group.

The right service headlight, blackout marker, brush guard, and siren are seen in this straight-on view from the front of the Grant. The support bar for the stowage bar is a T-bar fabricated by tack welding a vertical bar to the center of a horizontal bar.

Details of the mounting bracket for the left, sealed-beam headlight and blackout marker can be seen in this frontal view. On the hull behind the lights are two brackets for storing a machine gun tripod.

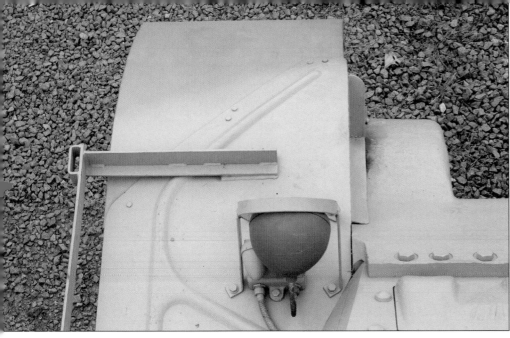

The stiffening pattern stamped into the stock M3 fender is clearly visible in this overhead view of the left front fender and sand shield. The end of the vehicle's left-side stowage rail can also be seen.

This overhead view of the right final drive housing shows that the first character of the casting number was partially cut off during manufacturing.

The barrel of the 75mm gun is on the left of this overhead view of the right front fender and sand guard. The end of the vehicle's right-side stowage rail can also be seen.

This view looking down at the fender to the front of the 75mm sponson mount shows that scalloped cuts have been milled into the front ledge of the sponson, in order to provide a thinner profile through which to bolt the sponson to the fender.

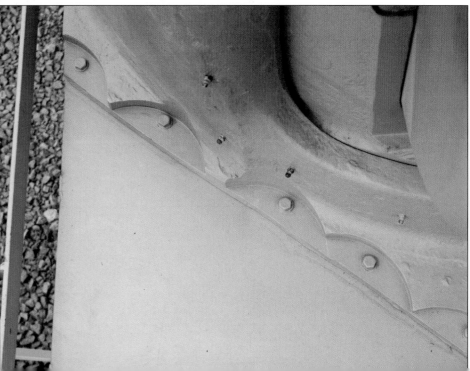

This head-on shot of the front of the 75mm gun mount shows the shields for the elevation and traverse rotors. Details of the hold-open brace for the driver's forward vision port are also evident. The lower end of the brace attaches to a bracket mounted on the outside of the vehicle.

The M2 75mm gun of the Grant was the shorter of the main guns installed in the M3 family of medium tanks, the M3 gun being the later and longer version. The bore of the gun is rifled with 24 grooves, right-hand twist. The barrel swells slightly towards the muzzle.

The protectoscope housing inside the driver's front vision port is seen here on the upper part of the front of the vehicle. Visible through the opening is the front of the turret basket and the front access opening.

The driver's front vision port is held open by a brace secured to the inside of the port and to the bracket on the vehicle's front visible in this photo. The splash guard molded into the glacis surrounds the sides and bottom of the port when closed.

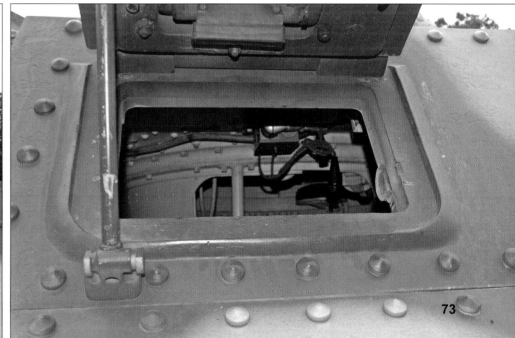

In the foreground of this overhead view is the driver's vision port. The protectoscope housing is mounted off-center. At the upper right in the background of the picture is the top of the siren.

The driver's side vision port appears at the center of this view from the roof atop the crew compartment on the left, front side of the upper hull. Visible below, on the outside of the hull, are the stowage rail and the vehicle's front left fender.

The closed-off port for the fixed .30-caliber machine guns is seen here from above, with the left final drive housing at the top of the photo.

A circular plate at the top of the 75mm gun sponson covers the upper traversing trunnion of the gun mount. Atop the plate, to the left of the gun, is the mount and guard for the gunner's M1 periscope, which traverses in unison with the gun. An irregularly-shaped splash guard surrounds the periscope mount. The roof hatch is to the right.

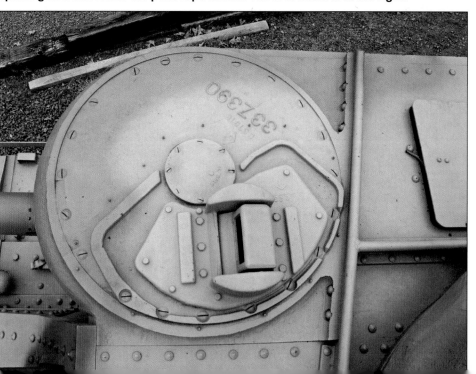

This frontal view of the top of the 75mm gun sponson shows the slight bevel ground into the front edge of the sponson roof. This design allowed a better downward field of vision through the gunner's periscope. Small studs surrounding the periscope splash guard facilitated attachment of a canvas cover over the periscope.

The driver's revolving periscope mount was an addition made to the Grant Cruiser tanks. The front base of the turret is to the left.

The rear deck of the Grant is seen here from the turret. A hand crank for manually starting the engine is lying at the rear of the deck. Brackets for pioneer tools and a tow cable are arranged around the deck.

Footman loops are found on all sides of the storage box fixed to the right rear of the hull. In a circular recess to the rear (right) of the two armored fuel filler covers is the knob that controls the shutoff valve for the right fuel tank.

Adjacent to the storage box, on the left rear of the vehicle, are three armored fuel-filler covers. The fuel shutoff valve knob is missing but its recess remains. The armored fuel-filler covers are for, bottom to top, the left inner fuel tank, left sponson fuel tank, and auxiliary generator fuel tank.

The turret is seen here from the left rear of the vehicle.

This look at the underside of the turret bustle reveals the casting surface textures, which range from fairly smooth to rough.

The varying textures of the cast turret are also visible in this side view. The welded seam joining the top and bottom sections of the turret is visible below the pistol port. A splash guard has been tack-welded around the base of the turret.

The turret bustle extends back beyond the turret ring, with the loader's pistol port located to the right. Turret armor thickness varied from 3 inches at front, to 1/25 inches on the roof. The rear, shown here, had 2 inches of armor protection. On the rear plate of the crew compartment, below the turret, is another pistol port with protectoscope (bottom right). The bowl-shaped antenna bracket, located on the left of the crew compartment, was not installed on all Grants.

The protrusion towards the front of the roof of the turret accommodates the internally-mounted 2-inch grenade launcher (called a "bombthrower" in Britain). The loader's pistol port is located toward the rear of the right side of the Grant turret. (Kevin Sharp)

The loader's pistol port is seen here from the rear of the turret. The upper and lower sections of the turret were welded together at the weld seam on the turret near the bottom of the pistol port.

The turret on a Grant is viewed here from slightly below the roof line of the hull. The opening for the grenade launcher (bombthrower) is at the top of the turret at the left edge of the photo. Next to the 37mm gun is the round opening for the .30-caliber coaxial machine gun. The shield plate assembly that contained those two guns, the sighting device, and the gun mounts was known as the M24 combination gun mount. In this example, some of the screws have been removed from the shield. (Kevin Sharp)

77

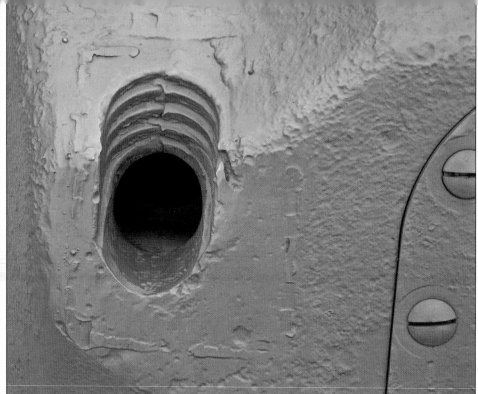

The Grant turret took up appreciably more roof space than the M3 Lee turret. This view shows the turret overhanging the front-rear roof stiffener, whereas the Lee turret came even with the left side of the stiffener. There were mounts for two radio antennas toward the rear of the turret roof but only the right antenna is installed on this tank. (Marc Sehring - National Museum of Americans in Wartime)

The left antenna mount is of a different, pedestal-style design that is bolted to the roof of the turret.

The grenade launcher featured a stepped design on the upper half of the opening. The gun shield (a corner of which is visible on the right) is held in place with slotted screws.

The right antenna mount on the turret incorporates a rubber boot with a tightening clamp at the top. The mount fits into a recess on the roof, to allow for the level placement of the mount. The loader's pistol port is visible below and to the right of the antenna mount. The rough texture of the turret casting surface is evident.

(Top) The Grant turret was designed with a bustle to accommodate the British No. 19 W/T (wireless telegraphy) set. Various controls were labeled in English and Russian for Soviet users of the set. The light bulb-like objects on the device are electrical connections. Below the set is a box for spare parts for the radio. Storage boxes for binoculars and hand grenades are located to the right.

(Bottom Right) The split hatch of this Grant's turret rotates on the screwed-on ring, and features a periscope mount.

(Bottom Left) The No. 19 wireless transmitter/receiver set can be seen behind its protective cage in the interior of this Grant turret, glimpsed through the commander's open hatch. The turret hatch of this particular Grant cruiser lacks the periscope mount. A plate has instead been bolted over the empty periscope-mount opening. On the rim of the hatch opening is a socket for a hand-operated, pintle-mounted machine gun. (The Tank Museum, Bovington, Dorset)

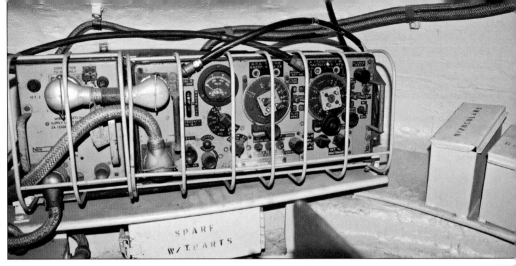

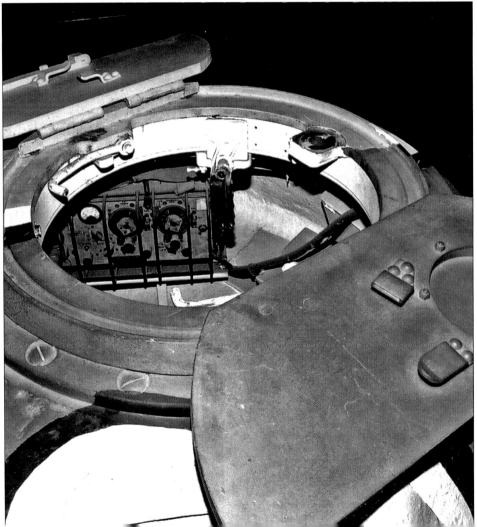

79

The recoil shield of the 37mm gun bears the nomenclature plate for the M23A1 combination gun mount fitted to this vehicle during its restoration. The correct mount for the Grant turret was the M24 combination mount, and this mount seems to be a later replacement. There is a clamp for a telescopic sight (not used on the Grant) toward the top left. The cylinder to the front of the recoil shield is the firing solenoid.

The Grant's instrument panel is of the standard M3 design. The large instrument on the left side of the panel is a compass. The oil temperature gauge has been removed from the center of the panel. To the left of the open vision port is a storage box for two spare protectoscope prisms. Below the instrument panel are the (disabled) fixed machine gun ports (left) and steering/brake levers. The vehicle nomenclature and serial number plate is the uppermost of the two data plates (far right).

The vertical cylinder of the gyrostabilizer system (right) is mounted near the Grant's 75mm gun's upper recoil cylinder. The stabilizer system's hydraulic lines and other components are missing. A casting links to the periscope mount and is connected to the gun mount's upper traversing trunnion. The casting allows the mount to traverse in unison with the gun. The link to the right of the periscope mount is attached to the gun elevating mechanism. It enables the periscope to tilt in unison with the elevation of the gun.

Sheet metal panels have been fastened with hex bolts and recessed grommets to the inside of the hull and side door on the right sponson to the rear of the 75mm gun mount. Details of the protectoscope mount are apparent. The curved rail to the left is part of the recoil guard.